# Frederick Pollack

# THE LIBERATOR

## SV

**SurVision Books**

First published in 2024 by
SurVision Books
Dublin, Ireland
Reggio di Calabria, Italy
www.survisionmagazine.com

Cover image from Dream AI prompt: "The liberator" by the author

Design © SurVision Books, 2024

ISBN: 978-1-912963-56-0

# Acknowledgments

Grateful acknowledgment is made to the editors of the following, in which some of these poems, or versions of them, originally appeared:

*Cerasus Magazine:* "Hope and Change"

*The Courtship of Winds:* "The Reward"

*Duality:* "DBA"

*Fleas on the Dog:* "Scherzo"

*Innisfree Journal:* "Yakety-Yak"

*Lost Boys Press E-zine (Straight on Till Morning):* "Return to Sender"

*Lothlorien Poetry Journal:* "Hand-me-down" and "Ripeness"

*Modern Poetry Quarterly Review:* "Prism" and "Effort"

*Mudlark:* "The Cactus," "Along Tenth," "The Day Room," "Appearing," "The Reward," "For P.," and "The Conference"

*Nauseated Drive:* "Eighth Seal" and "Ray of Entropy"

*Nine Mile:* "Session"

*Plato's Caves Online:* "Fifth Wall"

*Red Ogre Review:* "Spring Journey"

*Streetlight:* "Rembrandt Etchings"

*Sybil Journal:* "Figurine," "Ode," "Eighth Seal," "Also Thou Knewest It," "Last Words of Gramsci," *"Nachlass,"* "The Recruit," and "Night Table"

# CONTENTS

*The Impulse, ineradicable,*
*labours into life. Scrutiny;*
*manipulation toward some kind*
*of understanding; toward the Good.*
*The Process as it hath revealed*
*its Waste on high.*
    *Let our hate reach that.*

–Thomas Kinsella

*For Phylis*

## Nachlass

I'm not sure who it was. His mother
had boxes, bundles, frayed shopping bags full
of work, and humbly, tearfully begged me
to confront them. As I sorted,
red pencil in hand, she became not
his mother but his ravishing (exotic?)
wife/soulmate/enabler, with stories to tell,
the apartment no longer a mother's shrine
but the usual booklined burrow. I lost
my long white selfless wings but gained
attraction and intentions towards
the wife. But presently editors, scholars,
hovering, benign yet vampiric, blocked
his battered lamp. Had she summoned or
become them? Fierce grad students
pounced; I hadn't known him (or don't think I did)
but made something up, uncertain whether
any of this was happening …
The red pencil, there to send
gnarled stanzas, whole mad books to Parnassus
instead of the possibly more interesting
shelves of oblivion, didn't.

## Spring Journey

Two centuries today since the last android.
I remember them. I shared
the general – well-polled – dislike
of their unconvincing skin, stupidity,
and monotonous toneless desire
to please. Though of course I understood
the motive for these: artificial
intelligence mustn't progress
beyond a certain point. But I never
joined the debates
about consciousness, pain, selfhood,
"things with faces" ... cowardice, perhaps.

Now the vast machines
plough and sow the varied vegetable fields
along the road; a many-limbed
unit repairing
an irrigation sprinkler gleams in the sun.
Somewhere robots stand by controls
coordinating the planting;
somewhere a person sits
coordinating them. The friends I'm visiting
live far from me;
this annual drive is a ritual,
cherished among the many that make up life.

We seldom use the word "relationship";
one refers to specific couples, trios, networks
(and the occasional tragedy)
as nouns, paradigms,
and everyone knows what one means.

They greet me, Don and Shulamith,
with the superb liqueur
they distill. We stand on the verandah
watching my car quietly
come round the house and fold itself away.
A wind has risen; ducks bob on the pond.
The children have gone, to one or another town;
they left me, of course, their regards.
Then for an hour I admire,
in their wide-mouthed vases (whose potter
Don praises in detail), the arrangements.
A branch from one of the new, accessible
pines forms almost a circle,
symbolizing – smiles Shulamith –
my return, from their point of view, from a long
journey. Daffodils, tulips,
but mostly the bluestem
and other grasses. Some dusty twigs
representing grief at the kids' departure, with
a poppy for Acceptance.
Then, in stages, we eat.

A week with them. Other guests arrive:
musicians, a dancer,
a chef who rejects robot help. I read
from older work but mention
I'm trying to escape
the usual austerity, working on a long
emotionally varied
epic about a network. Which I'm not ready
to read. Someone jokes: if I'm not careful
I'll reinvent the novel.
(Not really funny – no one
wants to go back to all that.)
Driving home I envy
what my friends have made, and think how,
although my town is quiet, pleasant, stable,
I, too, may ... Beyond the fields
hills rise, then mountains,
and beyond them, all the way
to the Pole, places where others live:
wolves, bears, wolverines, polar bears,
the new birds.

## Last Words of Gramsci

*"Pessimism of the intellect, optimism of the will."*

I think that when my former students think
of me, they think I'm thinking
about them, and what I'm thinking
is what I should have said
the last day of the semester. And when
they formulate (or not) some
heroic-pessimistic slogan
like Gramsci's, above (which I've always
secretly disliked:
could it not also have been spoken
by a fascist?), a dim dirty pride
that they have never lived by it
appears in some; in others
a wish that they remembered what it was.

But what I want to have said or to say
now is Forget it, kids; you're off the hook.
(I taught creative writing, by the way.)
Though the world exists to be put into
a book (that's Mallarmé),
it isn't one you have to read, or write.
Let your career be your Idea
as Spengler said. And the resentment
I didn't start or help or dissipate
or focus may become
a poem – one poem, left for retirement.

## The Recruit

Cults multiply, even among liberals,
who are not immune
to the general secret yearning to be zombies
(free of the self and shame and capital)
and tend to disappear when they're alone.
I attend introductory meetings
of one of the few that let in Jews
as long as we aren't too overtly
you-know. Inept, like liberals:
after they set out
their creed, they actually ask
(instead of seducing me further) what I think.

"I'm prepared to agree,"
I say, "that the craziness
of the subatomic world doesn't end there.
That worlds and space itself are round and crowded
because we perceive them lazily, and what really
exists are floating visionary platforms,
yours over there, mine over here …
What I want to be sure
you accept is that my platform
is temperate and safe, with rolling hills,
vast cenotaphs of bigots, fools,
and the other unmourned, a table set
before me in the wilderness, and
when I tire, a well-appointed bungalow
with a view of the edge."

## Freight Elevator

In dreams you complain to the super about
your dreams. He tells you to
come down to the sub-basement,
we'll see what we can do. Doesn't
sound confident. One is never
alone in the padded cell of
such elevators. The milf
from 40B, her mascara smeared till
she's hoarse, and wearing
more than you're worth but also more
than she is, paces. Something shapeless
from 12A curls on the floor, crying
from what he knows are bourgeois problems
he deserves. Alone in the hypermodern
light of the Lowest Level, you stare
at warnings you pass: "Safety First."
"Zero Days Since the Last Accident."
"Poetry Makes Nothing Happen."

## Night Table

A dusty stack of urgent reading.
A learned journal, which
if finished would at last make one learned.
A lamp, too large for its space, but
an heirloom. Some old pill bottles that
may yet come in handy,
or reassure because no longer needed.
Near the edge, tonight's pills, awaiting water:
for sleep, for regularity, for
the heart. Considered as a still life
it would be a bad joke,
except in the sense that it's still life.

## Ripeness

It's possible that failure ends.
But you have to become it in time.
Too early, and youthful hormones
sour into rage;
too late, and heart lungs liver punish you.
Do it right and you find yourself,
as Marx said, proletarianized,
though without his promised change in consciousness:
your triumph a walk to the drugstore,
successful eradication
of mold from a shower curtain,
each meal, each check you can cover.
And the world you inherit
will be white strips of cloud
reinforcing sturdy grey,
like an advanced cardboard.

## Struggle

The time-storm that dropped them
on us also wrapped them
for a while in a field
(we saw it faintly swirl and spark)
that kept them from seeing or hearing us
beyond whatever stimulus
made them orate. We kept on talking
about and over them. Dr.
P. quoted Eliade,
who said when he met one in that era
that he had encountered the smell,
sweat and dirt, so often in India,
he wondered why a Western youth
would volunteer for it. B. meanwhile picked up
the little mess the time-storm
or any storm could make in her
spare neat vast beautiful apartment.
By now they had noticed the computer;
would they grasp, I wondered, the fulfillment
and ruin of their hopes, or was it
just alien horror? It didn't stop
the male with his spine-length hair from constantly
grinning and telling us what mushrooms
had taught him, something we needed to learn.
Or the girl, quite attractive (her peasant blouse
a multicolored spot amidst B.'s beige)
from saying she could see what we were –
profiteers if not warmongers –

and that they should split. "He doesn't listen," said B.,
with her usual irony. "It seldom
happened," said K., an artist, who seemed
attracted to them, "that you'd find
a mixed, political and … mystical couple.
They must have come from before the split."
"It wasn't I, it wasn't I,"
murmured P., the old professor,
tone hard to interpret. But the field
was fading; our ancestors saw
the truth, fell as silent
as B.'s rich husband A., who glared at them
with a disgust so deep it was almost love.

**Figurine**

One night a civilization
rises. Like all of them,
it begins with nomad thieves,
who luckily have many miles
of waste to speed around in, dust
to raise, agriculturists to spear –
heroes, in short. But something, a bacterium?,
obstructs the formation
of traditions, castes, values; when patriarchs feel
the need to beat a wife or extort
a neighbor, a whining infantile sleepiness
intervenes. Women say
what they want, do what they think, experience
doubt. Among children, proto-bullies
get sick, are let off chores, stay home,
as the culture matures, from school.
Visitors from all over
remark the civility
and peace of that country, the chronic look
of toothache or dyspepsia on its faces.

Art alone
compensates. Statues
of bearded psychotic warriors, not even legend.
Over time these grow
more intimate, stylized –
the line of the horse, the scimitar's curve
eventually as small as in
my original vision.

18

## Ode

Life-giving *Ambiguity,* which only
we knowers adore and others
ignore for as long as they can but which then
brings brittle denial and rage, causing breakdown
and tears in dependents; great Scales
that may or may not be of justice but
where power, to its dismay,
is weighed and found wanting; dark
Energy stretching the borders of truth
beyond starlight; convivial Grin
of art, however hostile; estranged
but hopefully reconcilable
sister of hope; our curse, our cloak, our work …

The thick white robe on a hook on the back
of the bathroom door takes on
a living shape: sleeve slightly bent
at the elbow, hem
swept back as if in motion, shoulder
sagged. Who will see it
(though probably not care to
inherit) when I'm gone? And is the mood one
of vanity or terror?

## Chronus

476: a villa near Ravenna,
where a firm, so to speak, is being dissolved.
"I wish," says the Master, dismayed
by awkward numerals and the countless
details of his estate, "we had computers."
"Or what comes after," says the Visigoth,
displaying his well-informedness
and Latin. "Those brain-chips."
They share a sigh, which extends to the fleas
the barbarian has to suffer, and the lice
everywhere on the Master – "pearls of God,"
according to that onerous, shared
convenience, the Church. A serving-girl
(her status shortly not exactly slave,
but secure) ungracefully refills
their thick and cloudy glasses.
I know her, thinks the Visigoth;
she'll sew for or perhaps be
Christina of Sweden, then an anti-vaxxer.
As she leaves, he slaps her broad bottom. The Master
frowns; they get down to business. "My main
concern, as you know, and that of my group,
is family." "As is mine," says the other,
"but there's no way to stop our coming in.
We're *hospes,* guests. The word 'hospitality'
is emerging to cover it." The Master wrinkles
his nose: "Intermarriage."
The chieftain shrugs: "Yes, but the current era
will seem like infancy – mythical, forgotten;

for them to trace your bloodline back to it
should suffice." "I trace it to Aeneas,"
growls the Master. "Or, now, to Melchizedek.
What counts – " he gazes after the girl,
eyes resting on the traditional whip
on a peristyle wall, "is control of labor."
"Word is," says his friend,
"that industry will come to this part of
the nation-state" (they both smile) "first.
It'll be bought out, of course, but our heirs won't suffer."
They drink. Oh poor magas, you're right
that history is all conspiracy; you are its tools.

## Eighth Seal

The end of days is not the end of nights.
In the sinister mild weather,
streetlamps haloed in mist, all the bars
are open, all human dealings in them.
But not all humans – in large part,
I suspect, they comprise
the packs of dogs and unaccountables
at large in the streets. Not rabid
except with freedom, they bounce haplessly
off legs, their cries
evocative of music I disliked;
perhaps when they calm down they'll want
to be petted. In the clubs
and joints, extortion graft and fraud
occur in radiance and *à haute voix;*
the suits, high end or low, involved in it
seem unaware of this or of their growing,
interested crowds. Wife-beaters,
abusers also seek,
helplessly, the spotlight. Out of shape though I am
(one's status, dead or living, undecidable)
I wipe the floor with them,
then chide those sweethearts who mourn and tend
for other than economic reasons ... Having drawn
incurious listeners, I hold forth
against a world of hurt

with, I'm afraid, the same dreary abstractness
as the already ignored, hovering
angels; and since there has to be an end,
accede to being transformed to a stuffed shirt.

## Ray of Entropy

Someday interrogations
will change:
the good and bad cop,
the fastidious sadist and his brute
colleague of the secret police
become tactful, polite.
They will let you out,
with a tentative pat on the back,
clean clothes, a chit for housing, food
and drinks, and the understanding that
you'll be called in again.
Outside, your skin tingles
from the end or lack
of beatings, and you see
in the expression and walk,
unsure of the ground's caress, of other
passersby that they too are free,
at least provisionally.
In a restaurant, you consider
then defer or let pass
the possibility of consciousness.
Resummoned, you find
your inquisitors at odds:
querulous, sniping; it has nothing to do
with you. At later meetings
there's even a therapist. In the end,
you think you won't show up again;
they just seem old,
like you, like the sky above the city.

## Also Thou Knewest It

Stumbling in memory
on a line by Montale:
*Anche tu lo sapevi, Luce-in-tenebri! –*

and finding myself moved;
almost, as one says, "upset" –
another memory accounts for it:

recalling in part with whom I spoke, not where;
impression of old wood, full shelves,
my taste but not myself belonging there –

accused of believing in nothing;
replying, "You talk about 'belief'
as if it were praiseworthy in itself."

## The Lower Town

The app misleads: the supposed sidewalk
is narrower than you,
and pathological small cars descend
the cobblestones. You hug
the interminably pissy
castle wall, identify
the niche where a duke once met
the clubs and daggers of his brother's bravos;
but the plaque to a resistant shot
by fascists seems gone.

When you've researched a place too much,
one of the pillars of tourism,
mystery, vanishes;
the other, safely not understanding
or belonging, trembles.
As when you finally reach flat concrete,
dodge trucks and cross to the dockside plaza
with its tables. Because you can pay
the waiter is pleasant;
you share a look with other foreigners
the natives wish away.

Only the sun is as promised.
Two or three vast yachts
of no particular nation, made
of the invulnerable new ceramics,
appear untenanted,

attended by the smaller craft
of the local mafioso, mayor, and banker.
Beyond lies the sea,
but you know what the sea has become.
Poets and the sentimental
should find, you think, another image
of culmination.

## Scherzo

Her scent lingered;
the soft voice left no echo but a thought.
Steps receded in a hallway
and in the tunnels of my ears.
It would be the moment,
I thought, for distant bells across rooftops
but it isn't that kind of place.
Outside, some blue remained –
royal blue, and clouds without contours.
I lay unmoving, relaxed, awake,
a trillion tiny symbiotes,
my inheritance from a billion years,
companionably working, death distracted,
until I wished her back.

A realm without an anthem;
the arms of each successive emperor
(who might as well be,
for all the good it did him, modern,
a dictator) is a musical phrase.
Which may be martial, boastful, furtive, choral,
it doesn't matter: he has no territory.
Tanks and investors sweep
at will across the land, at most
delayed awhile without maps or highways.

He likes, however, to confer
that which is his by right:
a moment – more for the most favored,
who remains the king of an afternoon
however the regime changed in the night.

## DBA

Someone besides dentists
must work in those sad shadowed Midtown towers
built in the 1910s. I receive –
rag paper, tasteful letterhead,
alchemical logo – an invite
from an unknown firm. They are offering me, they say,
the world, though fully cognizant
that as a poet I am myself a world.
Fighting traffic, crowds, and assumptive lack
of illusion I arrive on time. The office
is everything one could imagine:
caricatures and photos of our dead,
not all from cirrhosis, first
editions, dust. A courtly specter, full
of allusions to ancient scandals, shakes
my hand. They offer publication, generous (!)
royalties, tours, "though not, I'm afraid,"
(he smiles) "given current mores,
adoring coeds appearing in
your bed, as they did in Dylan Thomas's."
They're only asking me to change my style.
"Untypically," I say, "I've done some digging.
You're a wholly-owned subsidiary
of a conglomerate so vast, and whose
majority shareholder is so well-known
(among those who care) a pig, that
I must decline, as I would anyway."
At which the ceiling becomes morgue-light,
the walls recede, turn glass, the rolltop desks

into cubicles; he loses, if not age,
something like age, and makes the same offer:
"You believe your work will enlist,
if not the God you rule out, or
the masses, a less stylish dust
than we tempted you with, some ad hoc principle:
time, perhaps. But we've acquired it,
with space. Legitimate poets are firms,
their brand the anguish of their past, their income pity …
People are corporations, my friend."

## Long Haul

Often, in a nation on
the fringes of that nation
of liars believing each other,
we see or pretend to see
in the eyes of its authorities
(a governor re-outlawing masks
because freedom) a certain deadness,
though what is missing isn't life, exactly ...
Meanwhile the hospitals fill again;
nurses intubate,
and later close the eyes of
men who curse them, who deny
they have it and that having
lost they have ceased to exist
in the eyes of that nation
of gamblers ... And again
the nurses tell themselves their strength will last
another day or round or hour,
though they know this too
is a kind of denial. While in
corridors, among patients
with other problems (some who never
quite recover), here and
there the homeless lie:
those who quietly cry
for contact; those
who die alone, refusing to be touched.

## Dark House

Guilt last night for not having
called Mother in so long;
relief on waking with her dead.

## Harmless

He was somehow *damaged.* Enormously
careful not to step on people,
he stayed within police lines, leaned
on an upper-story setback. Tired,
he squatted, then sat on and cracked
the street, snapping lampposts.
(Seemed unaware of this; no one made
an issue of it.) Asked to move
to the Park, he sighed, stood,
walked gingerly – the effect,
among the hundred convoying police cars (one
could tell he disliked the sirens), strange.
Behind him repairs began. He sat
again, on a cleared area, knees
up. He liked to talk to people
when the cops let them through (at first they didn't,
which distressed him). Scientists
wondered how he modulated
that Voice. But what people heard
when he leaned down to them was as
inane as what most of them said. And when
they poured out their hearts, or asked why
he had come, Who sent him, was he The One etc.,
his responses seemed inadequate;
what they mostly remembered was the Face,
ingenuous, somewhat tearful, filling the world.

Those who hung back, reflecting what
they might say or beg, caught on fast (or had
as usual expected nothing),
and drifted off or stood around, their thoughts
the sort that wind like snakes around other voices.

## Dufy

Still, in his seventies, the smile without agenda;
the exemplary suit, though its cut now
of New York, not London – as the tan,
he said, was from Arizona …
an effect of sunlight in this Breton gloom
and freshly-flowered, long-unpainted room.
But the Countess remembered his hands from before;
they were at ease now, fingers straight.
"A new treatment – it's largely why I went.
Much easier now to hold a brush!"
The husband, a director of companies
that might yet revive, had little knowledge of art;
found an opening here, and talked till the painter
was bored (of course not showing it)
about illness and age.
He knows about us and the Germans, the Countess
realized, the later unpleasantness;
won't mention it … though during dinner,
which was redeemed by the wine, Dufy asked
about a daughter whom he well remembered
and they had to work around a silence (hers) –
"She's studying." And speaking of his own
experience: "I stayed mostly in the South,
wound up in Vence. But since I
was neither a Jew, nor poor, nor political,
they left me alone."

In the painting, the marigolds and asters
rule; they seem to invest
the sideboard, fresh and gleaming as the walls,
which are, however, blue. Since the view
didn't interest him, the window is omitted.
The director is a patch of grey
hair, seen from behind, making a gesture
that could be witty. The daughter is there,
grown up as the painter imagined. She doesn't
resemble the Countess, nor the Countess herself;
they are bearers of one vivid red
dress, a stripe on the other, and a certain hazy
yellow. "I hope," the Countess said
in a farewell moment, "if you portray tonight,
you will show us as happy." He smiled:
"I will make you as happy as you can be."

## Godot

And again I give you another chance …
As if all the basic pairs
that precede selection of an actual victim –
boss and thug, unequal lovers,
epigone and master, artist and arsonist,
the alien who seeks and the one who hides –
were choices, and positions could be reversed.
And again you, I, or both of us
are standing in a dead zone, and I dream
of a return of phone booths –
they don't have to be red and quaint, just functional –
to all the wastes and forests of the world.
Then I wouldn't have to send
a handy, otherwise abandoned child
to tell you I'm not coming; I could call.
Even now, as you rephrase
obsessively your impermissible pleas,
I think how I'd reply –
though the voyage from word to word is like crossing
from stone to stone a difficult stream,
triumphing with each step, keeping one's eyes
down so as not to see no other shore.

## Sub

It doesn't need to refuel –
could stay midsea miles deep for five more years.
But here it is at 0100 hours,
silently entering its pen.
Something – a person, chip, or document –
must be going aboard
or waits to be brought ashore, perhaps under guard
or in a bag. Aware there will be no leave,
and of the moment when the vessel stops,
crewmembers wake or sleep
according to their schedules and their duties.
Outside, tropical heat,
untropical styleless American structures.
The town for the most part sleeps
but somehow knows that the sub and
its missiles have returned.
As if its reactor fueled
the music in some places,
the arm raising a cue,
gun, fist, or open hand,
the day's recorded sermons on two stations,
the obedient words of children
up for some reason.

## But the Fire

Christmas. Up early for no reason.
Solid overcast, which splinters,
dissolves like a mistake;
it's going up to 70 today.
People like warmth, warmth is being given them.
The omicron variant (how quaint that will sound)
keeps you home. You'd like to follow tradition
but have streamed the only films that weren't imbecile,
and will have to order in, if they're delivering.
The phone rings; robocall. Tomorrow, at least,
machines won't sing
about presents to the poor, home to the exiled,
warmth in winter. Desperate for stimulus,
you seek un-feelgood news. Floods in the heartland:
boats snagged on cars, kids clutching sodden dolls,
weeping. Send ten dollars
despite reluctance to waste sympathy
on that other, the Trump species.

## Seedtime

What we all really wanted back then
was dignity. No,
let's not be sentimental. Some could care less,
which means, significantly, couldn't. Some
would have no idea what I'm talking about
now, as they didn't then. And some,
myself included, found it easier
playing the fool, wanting dignity.

Not respect. Respect comes from others,
of whom there were already
too many. Good parents confer it, but dignity
can threaten even them. Respect
gets watered down
into popularity, likes, and what gangsters expect.
The other comes from an unclear source
to an obscure recipient. Then you have it,
even if you're kicked
and laughed at as you crawl in your own vomit.

Loners pursued it. Loners read difficult, printed
books. There are no loners anymore,
only the social self, a brute
capable of anything.
What passes for loners, however many
people they shoot, are still just trying to belong.

## Exiles' Café

The party is always on. Ovid and Brecht
hold court; Dante remains standoffish
but shows up, with Miłosz; Hugo
offers counsel to newbies;
Cernuda and Khodasevich, known
behind their backs but fondly as
"the guitar and domra," entertain.
Sutzkever and Celan
look in. The crowd of police and secret police
outside forever in the freezing rain
are sometimes treated to a single drink
by an elegist inside; fight over it.
Eventually, a year or two from now,
an American appears. Gets into it
with someone Putin hounded.
Though where both met their end was bad,
our boy or girl's undoubtedly traumatic
exposure to lockup, "Jesus Training"
etc., can't – this seems the consensus –
compare to the late Russian's
acquaintance with rococo poisons.
(Or else they're just being snooty Europeans.)
Time passes, though the immortals
don't age. One night someone enters
who stops the talk. It's hard to tell
either the given or intended gender,
age, the proper weight upon
those bones, even the color of its eyes.

It stands there, breathing unaccustomedly,
uttering through distorted lips
noises perhaps meant to be a poem.

## Bash

There is a festival I can't quite grasp;
likewise the architecture,
except that it agrees with Adolf Loos
that decoration is sin, and is madly sinful,
and colored like those shacks in Buenos Aires ...
But a Square is a Square, even without
a church (let someone else provide the bells!)
or statues of generals, and crazed dancers
are dancers, and every culture has
its blintz, pierogi, or dim sum – they're all here,
handcrafted and delicious like
the music. The holiday seems
to have begun with decadence, to commemorate
no event, no triumph
(except, perhaps, that of
an abstraction). But it invents traditions:
the retrofuturistic shoulderpads,
challenging gowns, masks eagerly removed,
while beneath its drums and smashed guitars the music
has something aristocratic ...
Some folks misbehave, are as vulgar
as if they or any of it were real,
but they get gently taken off somewhere
to sober up and feel apologetic.
Later, behind windows, possibly curtained,
around the plaza, costumes are doffed
for what all festivals are really about;
and sometimes in the early morning couples
stroll amidst the busy outsized roombas.

## For the Webb Telescope

Please, please, I beg you, I know you'll try,
though as I write at any moment
a garbled signal or small fast stone
can destroy
my hope among others ... Deploy
your eighteen golden mirrors
servomotors will labor
to make perfectly level, the vast and fragile
sunshield to keep you cool; and may you
retain enough fuel
securely to orbit
that distant point ...

It's the sort of specific, low-grade prayer
a saint among the dead might make,
if the dead wished anything.

For you see, I've given up
the hope of a message, either way,
or Friends coming; but know that
besides the earliest black holes
you'll be able to see
almost the surface of worlds,
whether they have seas,
and air
that something vaguely like myself could breathe.

## Yakety-Yak

Son (if I may call you that –
it guarantees my unimportance),
you shouldn't assume
that because my generation lived
before electrons, we weren't linked
to the World-Spirit, or didn't feel
the essential, defining,
disgust, or lacked friends. My gang,
for instance. Van, the other genius,
whom I could talk to, as hobbled by "acting out"
as I by timidity. Jack,
whose every blurted sentence strove
for enthusiasm; we accepted him out of
what might have been compassion. And Don,
who said I was the leader
because I was the biggest. *Happy* family – a bourgeois
in waiting, though he neither enthused nor theorized
about it. He had, however, a guitar.
All still virgins. (I've read that your cohort
is leery about sex; that's understandable but
regrettable.) A major thought of mine
that year was that by now I'd given up
on the idea of friends, now I only wanted
to fuck; would life always grant me
the previous, soured wish? And we
were white – so white – (you probably got that,
though you might have found it hard explaining
exactly what was lacking; we were, of course,
all pro-Civil Rights.

I'm sure you have a lot of close Black friends.)
One night, nothing happened. We pissed against
the rear wall of a church, walked back
onto California Avenue. None of us drove.
Surrounding streets had the names
of colleges; we lived there. Jack
raved solo about Tolkien; we never mentioned
his mother's drinking. Van sought municipal sawhorses
to displace, but the street was in perfect shape;
he then said something disparaging
about Kennedy, which set us off awhile.
I can't describe the whiteness
and silence of that street at midnight, though
its major colors were beige, and
residual pink and charcoal. My thoughts –
perhaps this will be true of you someday –
communicate across eons:
I think how at the start one feels
unequal to the world and at the end
to the young; it's the same feeling, as
I might with greater genius have known then.
At any rate, a cop
gauged without tension
our color, sobriety, clothes, and number
(submissiveness a given), reminded us
of curfew, and let us go. Two of us are still going.
But what sticks in my mind
is how Don, seeing the car
approach from the end of the street, strummed and sang,
"Mister policeman, don't arrest me, 'cause I just wanna wail."

## Things Change

We defeat them at last
by methods that make no one happy
but them least.

That fall you go on leave.
Someday the seasons
will separate again. There's a breeze.

The word "comrade," from the dust,
for want of any
other relationship.

You discuss the new vaccines,
interesting findings
in several fields, the hard line, the

emotions which, like bones,
go to nourish
the new forests.

## For Thomas Kinsella

*1928 – 2021*


A visually striking, largely joyless
environment. Jokes like coughs, one filthy city.
Priests deciding what the radio tells;
the slaughterhouse too near;
so much that isn't, can't be, said,
which may in fact be an ideal state
for poetry. A river runs through it
bearing many objectionable things;
the task is to remember them,
turning away, keeping an appointment
with one who looks at you and doesn't speak,
or does. Her eyes, her flesh are tired
but *the* flesh, never. File,
cross-reference; despite
a lying medium, not lying, ever.

## Along Tenth

A strong, fortyish fellow (bit of a gym-rat,
in fact) wasted time
saving his work, then walked down thirty floors,
neither having occasion
to help anyone nor be helped. Coughing,
disoriented by
the dust, he made his way slowly
across the plaza. Jumpers
struck near him, then the North Tower fell.
Too preoccupied to remember
wife, kids, or phone, he walked the eighty blocks
to his condo. He wasn't religious,
and his work had involved
trade, dangers to and costs of,
in many parts of the world, so his focus
had always been on that. What he thought of
("saw") during this walk wasn't
vengeance – that would be
a minor, ongoing part of it –
or a growth in understanding (though
some phrase like that occurred to him);
he understood things. No, what he saw
was a beautiful, transparent,
rotating cloud. In which those who were eaten
knew they were food, and didn't mind, and loved
the mouth, and were loved in return; so that
whatever hate they had to feel
was a mere seed or skin. He saw crowds
dying in grace. He was among them;

so was everyone he passed,
and he almost embraced and spoke to them.
But the love of his wife
and kids when he reached home
distracted him (he also found he was hungry).
The marriage solidified, work returned,
and in three years he developed asthma.
Faiths bloom every moment
in the shadow of what used to be
the imagination; some few flourish.

## The Day Room

Outside, a sullen wind forms
the dust of leaves from many autumns
into a fervid vortex like
Malczewski's "Melancholia" – but his figures
were martyrs, poets, heroes, while yours
are the usual. Their stupidity is such
they can't see you through the window. Which
may change, but for now
you're a bystander, next to the real;
what is real for a bystander
is fear. The room behind you
is big, bright, clean, quiet,
exempt. Though at your back
stands one who could lock your arms, snap your neck,
or summon those who would, for the moment
he's invisible, kind.

He wonders what you see and you're smart enough
to answer, A bird, and describe it;
then wreck it by saying He likes snow,
if only as a diversion
from chronic near-starvation.
And the one behind you mildly asks
how you feel about the people
out there. They must be mad, you say,
to be abroad in such weather,
but are warmed – fired – by a shared
desire to be alone,
sovereign, king and chief rapist

each of his tiny country, obeying
no law except those cleverly disguised
as instinct. As I recover, I've learned
theirs is the vital bond.

And he would answer, counsel, chide,
rephrase, but behind him
at the big table a patient
formerly in the health field weeps, an artist
describes at length how a new, gross
parody of an old, subtle
parody will make her career,
a poet crosses out and crosses out
lines already heavily crossed and decides
that's the poem, while others protest
the hurtful presence of those
who think themselves superior. Your keeper turns.
The bird is still there – pecks and finds
some frozen thing. Its eye
meets yours a moment, helping to resolve
the Problem of Other Minds.

## Appearing

Parmenides, appearing
in a distant future, looks as he did
to Raphael, stern and forceful. He ignores
ephemera, smog, cellphones, tyrants,
asks only two questions: How might I eat?
and Where might I
be relatively safe? – not out of pragmatism,
but because physical needs
are part of fate, which has always already happened.
He endorses Einstein's partial endorsement
of him, refutes Smolin
with math he picked up somewhere. Which sets
some scientists running; others
talk eagerly with him, although
it's hard since he omits the future tense.
"Spacetime is a block. Yes, there's a sixth great extinction.
No, we all die from fire, thirst,
and drowning. The successor species
evolves from rats. They don't
have time to develop fully, but are pleasant enough.
Joy exists elsewhere, but generally
one's smart enough to keep it to oneself."
One of the scholars (Parmenides
doesn't catch the name of her field) is as lovely
as the nameless goddess he invoked. "I suppose,"
he says, eating takeout,
"you want to protest my patriarchal
loathing of process." "Not at all," she replies.

"I only wonder
why the poem that contains us
has summoned you in person, not just your idea."

## The Reward

The reward of the historicist
is to read obsolete poems
on JSTOR and become
the poet's new best friend by buying him drinks.
It's summer, the cloudy ale
almost cool from its cask. The tide
recedes, the Thames stinks,
but only the historicist notices.
A sergeant-major obviously off
to the colonies wipes
his mustache on his wrist,
emotions reconstructable though complex
like those of the whores outside.
The poet loosens neither tie nor vest,
both worse for wear. He has
a week before a horse-cab, less
absurd than a colleague's fall from a bar-stool,
beats syphilis to him. Opinions
about darkies and Israelites are there,
but pleasantly subordinated to
despair. He accepts being questioned
however rudely
by a chap from the future, especially when
the latter relates how revered the work
will be, taught in schools; rattles off
the titles of critical studies. Sated,
dabbing away
a tear, the poet
asks questions of his own, untypically

(from all that is known of him) generous. No war
with France, he is assured; the new,
more distant enemy turned aside,
replete with retailed colonies; balloons
filling the air, a Workers' Earth ... The pub,
the river, poet, sergeant, whores
and endless clop and cursing fade
again into the quietness around
the historicist, who has no love for pain.

## The Cactus

Was it perhaps a mini-stroke?
My previous mild silence
in social situations, only broken
by anodyne male grunts often enough
to keep me accepted, has turned
to humor. Drawn from the dusty
abandoned frontiers of learning, twisted tales
from Continental philosophy
(some continent or other), and other cultures,
especially those with bigotries. Turkish joke
about the Laz, a minority along the Black Sea;
it involves buttocks. Setup requires
three scholarly minutes, puts listeners into
a kind of mental weightlessness
or blank-tank, perhaps perceiving
personality as a quantified waste of time.
Then there's my Aztec one. Aside
from eating people, Aztec society
was repressive and censorious. But if you
made it past sixty (few did), they let you
sit around, blind drunk on pulque,
insulting passersby. So one geezer says

## For P.

Amazed that you don't recall
the risk of breaking an axle
on our impossible descent into
that impossibly pink canyon
at Sedona.

And you, that I'm blank about
a great-aunt's last appearance
at some niece's bat mitzvah;
while neither of us is sure
in which Latin city …

You, likewise, your cellphone, me
the *other* notebook or my pills,
but that's how it goes:
if you forget, I remember;
if I forget, you remember.

## The Conference

Though jetlagged and grimy, I'm not driven
to the hotel to shower, sleep,
and schmooze with fellow poets, but to
a windowless grey basement. Beneath
a swinging hanging bulb I confront
what looks like the criminal element
though it insists it's official. "You're here
for the Conference," says the boss,
an obvious sociopath; asks in their language
if I speak the language. I don't,
"but I love some of your classics. In
translation," I burble, naming names;
he points out with a smile that they're all dead.
"Using what you know of our culture,
I'd like you to adopt the point of view
of one of our poets. What would he
or, excuse me, they write about?"
The picture on the wall behind him
may be the Palace or some mall. "Well," I say,
the poets at your universities
are probably linked to the international
avant-garde, which currently tends – " He shifts
in his chair, exposing a .38. "Otherwise
I'm sure they write about their grandparents
and parents," I go on, "if they're around, or
if not, depending on why they aren't;
and ... cows, and your beautiful scenery,
and endlessly about childhood – " One
of the goons makes a slapping gesture

as if missing a cosh. "And what do you think,"
asks the chief, "is the underlying theme of
these poems?" Insofar as a madman
can ask a serious question, this one is,
and I ponder a moment. "'Don't hurt me.'"

## Exchange

Man dies; the animals return,
changed. Following
the advancing season and small game,
a bear investigates a formerly barren
and Canadian cove. So does,
from the other side of the shore,
a whale. They regard each other.
"I was once something like you,"
says the whale. "I get that,"
says the bear. "You seem to eat well."
The whale projects a shrug. "Things are improving ...
still wouldn't invite you in. How's your side?"
Feeling that, after all, he's revealing
no exploitable secret, the bear describes
his expanding range. Adds,
mechanically, "At least they're gone." The whale
nods with his tail. They chat awhile,
comparing hazards, mating, meals,
abiding the difficulties
of using the word "I" to mean one's species.

## Who's Who

Don't worry about
the untraceable. In
whatever absurd state
they wound up, watching Fox no doubt,
they thought of you. Not as
a song without words, or even
an abandoned shrine
in the expanding desert, more as the punchline
of a private joke no one they knew
would get. But rest
assured: in dreams
the one who kicked you out or rejected
your offer vacates
a desk or bed. While one
you meet in fact again after thirty years
has nothing to say. A strange robed grinning
figure raises two
fingers in silly blessing and says, "Time."

## Scepter

Never obtrude, never impose –
his (though gender was moot by this point)
voice was also like that,
crushed by the contradictions:
wanting to whisper, but to make
the listener strain to hear would be impolite.
Likewise his treasures: a partly transparent
orange toothbrush,
a tiny pasteboard jewel
that might have come from giftwrap,
an old but undistinguished wooden box,
two inches on a side, he wouldn't open.
It can't be said he displayed these things
but he didn't hide them: the terror and
ambivalence lay in whether
they would lose or gain by being touched;
then came a burst of faith that I wouldn't take them.
Instead I agreed that the interior
of the transparent portion
of the toothbrush was a mysterious world,
like amber; that it lent interest
to anything behind it. That the jewel
was beautiful, or a reminder of beauty.
Visibly relieved when I stepped back
from the things, he suddenly announced
that God is not what people think:

not omnipotent, rather the weakest thing,
in flight from everything, possibly almost beyond
help or compassion;
his features firm, the voice inaudible.

## Safe Word

How often, amid the ruined lives
of others, did I clear
a place for myself to lie and read
my book on a stained
rug, littered floor (littered
not with drug paraphernalia,
stained not with blood, just the dreck
of other young should-be-professionals
overthrown by disaster within or without).
Once it was Barth's essay
on the *Epistle to the Romans*. I was researching
ideas I would never share, voices
firm, even poignant as long as you grant
the premise, which I didn't. It was a kind
of escapism more instructive
than the science fiction of my youth,
thrillers now. T. was out, looking for work,
his high-school brilliance undimmed but soured,
M. preparing dinner with what they had.
The flat looked out on an airshaft.
I wasn't a third, they were barely a couple.
She told me she had discovered
with another woman the delights of S&M.
Restraints, the whole bit. Her face
lit up as she spoke – a certain gentleness.
It occurs to me now: we still
had time
and the body's propaganda that things would work out.

## After a Funeral

No one I liked
particularly, but
one has to show support,
observe tears, listen to adult
children's stories, calculate

years, symptoms, chances, types
of love; observe
the surrounding stones with their little stones,
the green mat briefly covering
the box; come home, sleep badly.

Probably this is the usual
dawn light, unusually seen:
fingers of it across
a soiled window, the sliding screen
over half the window opaque

with dust. I should
go out with squeegee, spray,
ladder, rags, one remembers how
to climb and clean but
it's cold and I no longer must.

## The Treehouse

But where? A copse
of low-status trees
*beyond* the cul-de-sac, separated
by a fence then a wall from the highway.
(The houses Nixon Ford Dole Bush McCain.)
A father to build it, and a self
handy with nails.
Occasional condoms on the forest floor,
few bottles, no needles. And what occurred
up there? The cigarette
that was (that still is) adulthood. "Bonding"
( – reaching, here): emotions
surging, totalizing, ultimately normative;
ideological training.
Girls, perforce invited or demanding
access, deplored
male lack of connection with things and brought
– what? – fabrics? ...
Gone now. The nights filled

with serial killers.
Xbox healthfully
instructed one how to be king
of the galaxy or ruins.

The boards have fallen, warp beside the trees,
not worth return, hardly nostalgia ... while
for me (both "flats" and "apartments"
significantly named) there are
degrees of the impossible;
only the lowest easily imagined.

**Redshift**

They mention that the universe
at the largest scale resembles
a brain. ("They" being scientists,
who are friends, though they must translate
crudely to speak to you.) Skeins
of galaxies mirror those
of dust *within* galaxies, which echo
nerves – a fractal structure (which
we won't go into here because
the implications are unsettling).

Hard upon this discovery comes
another: the most distant,
most swiftly departing clusters talk
to you most easily. Well, not
the farthest, because of course they're
the first, and what they say (what
minds warmed by them say) is
naive, sometimes earnest, funny-
crazy, less communication
than play. It's those

somewhat nearer (though still exiting
fast), from before
the archaea, even the prokaryotes,
who chatter constantly. Who say you needn't
have hurt, in either sense, so much,
that your terms were never
precise, nevertheless

they adore you; but although there's endless
time for you to reciprocate, it's
all somehow wrapped up in goodbye.

## Hope and Change

In his third year back home,
Paul's sleep became troubled.
Small pleasures – showering off
each night the stink of Wendy's, possible
promotion there – had begun
to loom larger. Upstairs
his parents, both better employed,
continued like him to avoid sinking
towards Fox. Some weeks –
when Biden came in, when numbers of deaths dropped
that spring – they hoped. Few quarrels:
Paul was working, it wasn't his fault. But
one night he was confronted by
a presence. It seemed surrounded
by incomprehensible things: cows, mud,
thick ragged dirty woolen clothes,
lice. It stared at Paul and crossed itself,
and spoke. All nouns had gender, and genders
had many rules, were very distinct, but Paul
understood. He tried to explain
his laptop and the other things in
the basement. An urgent question involved
his priest. – I'm not very religious. – Who is
your lord? – Paul talked about Wendy's,
money, his hopes for at least
junior college. The figure's attitude
changed: relaxed, adopted
a dismissive grin. Addressed Paul
as son. I too have longed

to abandon the land like you, run off to the forest!
It's a good life, lazing about, if you don't weaken.
But watch out for the Companies.
– The Companies? echoed Paul. The somehow familiar
face darkened: Bad men
who do the work of the lords
with their own terrible joy, and for their own reasons.

## Wrong Floor

The elevators were out again.
The little card beside them typically
went on too long and painfully
about how often those in the Projects
are broken; at least ours don't reek,
often, of urine.
(No one reads these.) As I climbed I passed
the closet where I once received
for a fee the notes that let me pass
exams. (Behind its No Admittance sign,
it is only ever used for this purpose.
Farther up, of course, is the vaulted, airless
Exam Room itself.) Out of breath, I found
the right office. His secretary
challenged me. Yes, I said, I had
an appointment, had had one for eternity
or at least since before she was born. She was
afraid he was still busy;
I took a seat. After several hours
battling a hostile computer and callers,
her hair was frayed and we felt, I thought,
a certain solidarity,
though she was among the employed. My job
(I said when she idly asked) is to sit
in rooms like this, sensing
from their specific void the character
of bosses behind doors;
in another world they might be useful. Unable
to wait any longer, I said "I'll be back," and

descended two floors. How often,
like the guys in there, carefully never
conceding each other, one has to
wash the minimum at trickling sinks,
maybe beg
a razor; clothes and drycleaning
are of course another matter.
When I got back the office was closed.
I had felt I had more hours
in me, stood disoriented while
shifts changed and halls and stairwell filled
with people rising and sinking.
Suits grazed and tore the wall notices,
which said, in an attempt at classic style,
*Not only I shall be effaced*. Abruptly
tired, I thought of seeking a bunk
in the barracks under the roof. I could just
afford it, but deciding I was
more hungry than sleepy, returned to the lobby.
There a large poster
proclaimed in tiny print that the individual
is sovereign but his/her/their
desires are contradictory. Though we
ignore these notes we get sick of them, but
they're art. Outside, beneath
the vast tarp of the sky, the food trucks stretched
forever along the avenue. I bought
a taco. Tried to merge
with folks out there, who glared at me, thinking
that coming from inside I too was
the enemy. They eat badly, are often bulbous.
The bulk, I thought, of the population.

## Rembrandt Etchings

From however far away,
*detail.* The lovers, almost fully clothed,
amid bushes, her round blonde face
delighted, hopeful.
The returned Prodigal, kneeling,
embraced, exhausted – such
precision of apology and joy –

but seen by whom in the middle distance,
that fascinating distance you don't notice?
A bystander, a passerby
who stops to take the scene in wholly.

As in Christ Presented to the People
so they may choose between the thief and him:
steps, platform, doorway, every window full,
spear-carriers, hangers-on, all known;
and Christ, thorned head down, looking
tired, as one does after a beating,
caught likewise by the moment, with nowhere to go.

## Process

I was trying to be generous, humane, to construct
a rather pathetic, even sordid
figure, meanwhile deflecting
(entirely mentally, abstractly) the protests
of its supposed cohort: that it, they,
didn't want my pity, that I could never
imagine, that where I at best
saw pathos they saw strength; and I,
again subjectively, replied that pity
had not been my intention, rather
a sort of scaffolding from within which
understanding might be built;
                              and they
inquired firmly how this lazy,
counterfeit compassion differed, if
at all, from what an exploiter might
in a sentimental mood allow
himself to feel and praise himself for feeling;
                                              but
by now my attention was solely on
that scaffolding, a potentially
good image in a poem with none. It had
exceeded what the most boastful business
tower or whole financial centers
require; filled the sky, all skies, with
(amidst the dust and noise of drills)
a generalized anguish taking shape.

## Leave

In that city, far behind the lines, safe
from bombing, and where sublime
Intelligence prevents sabotage,
troops of all the warring parties
encounter each other. But something in the water
(it must be) precludes conflict. Uniforms
are clean, flesh purged of battle, images
of fallen comrades dulled in the mind. Photos
of wives, kids, girls are compared (or it may be
husbands, lovers, for these armies are modern;
in some the uniforms are – neatened – rags).
Soldiers find they admire each other's
disciplined or lackadaisical
step, irony or innocence, earthiness or urbanity
they would otherwise despise. In
the brothels everyone's considerate; in fact
there are no brothels, only love. And a surprising
number of peasant conscripts find themselves
enjoying under chandeliers the noise
of harpsichords and brooding flutes, or pictures
of boating parties, meadows without craters,
if not of generals and widows past.
Intellectuals in that town are all
about communication and the holiness
(if they use the word) of the human face
authentically perceived; and often,
under their auspices, lieutenants or sergeants
with different shoulder-flags chat over beers
at sidewalk tables. Till through the genial

haze they discover irreducible
priorities, of scripture, color, gender, and always
self or other; and mildly (it must be something
also in the beer) shake hands and
return, not quite reluctantly, to the front.

## Prism

Nothing has mystery
where there's no curiosity. The tourist
stays in a midrange airbnb
some blocks from the waves. After
settling in he's in costume:
pressed shorts, black knee-high socks (although
he scuttles swiftly, without cart or cane),
and proper wizened form. He rents
a midsized hybrid, twice a day
drives the length of the Avenue to eat
at the famous places. He enters
(from the street, it isn't difficult) the garages
of condos, where the building's mighty
pillars show; exhibits
a mild but allover thrill, feeling, sniffing
the crevices in the concrete, rusting
rebar. (Streets are often awash, vehicles
leave wakes; he savors
perversely the flood in his sneakers.) On various
pretexts he attends
board meetings, nods as residents
protest projected meddling and expense.
But mostly he walks the sixty or twenty
yards of sand between towers and sea,
smiling at bathers, his gaze
turning from pitted walls and relaxing
balconies to the waves
and back. Enjoying

a double vision, the beach overlaid
with those same towers, half- or wholly submerged,
lying on each other, some remarkably whole;
for gods remain godlike, even when decayed.

## Fifth Wall

Before poetry I failed at novels. Sex scenes
are hard to write, and otherwise characters
only wanted to *think;* I had to whip
myself and them back to the plot, which
bored me like any duty. Then came a time
when I thought of writing plays. But they bunched,
my characters, stage right or left,
orating. I made sure to mention
the gun early; when it was fired no one cared.

But what if I'd stuck with it? Rain
descends on a city I haven't seen
since childhood, a neighborhood full
of the bistros, galleries, and guilty joy
of gentrification. If the rain turns to snow, we'll
lose half of them at intermission. I sit
beyond hope or tension. Someone I
don't know but have somehow charmed gets up
to introduce my piece. Thank you all for coming.

## The Wreathed Skull

A polished skull on the same desk
as one's computer, wires, backup and all
the other prostheses doesn't
compute, is too discrepant to be
a symbol of anything. If I placed
a gold wreath on its brow, it might
direct more attention to itself, but people
would think I meant to honor another poet
(I don't know whose skull it was ...
he had all his teeth), or
myself (the very thought gives me a headache),
or death. Which I don't. I'd be happy, actually,
with laurel, but how does one get it? Or *make*
a wreath? So I use bay leaves,
carefully pierced and threaded, which lend
a kitchen rather than a charnel air
to my room. Meanwhile a cart creaks
outside, a peasant curses, touched
however faintly by the dreams and reason
of the Renaissance (I slip back when working);
he hasn't yet had time for new
fanaticisms. Someone comes
to clear the capon bones I strew
on the floor while typing.
She wraps them, muttering, in a rag, bears
them off ... Someday they'll rebel.

## Hand-me-down

We'll ignore what the former "middle classes"
(even they abandon the term)
get into when things get really bad;
it does its job, excusing bloodshed.
Those literates who are still extant
and talking revive, in a big way,
"past lives." An influencer says
we do remember them, it's just denial,
a willful mental fog that blocks them out.
The good news is, surviving readers read
more history, the bad is that it's all
dumbed down. An Epstein type,
exposed and hounded, says he was once
the "Walter" of *My Secret Life,*
Messalina a foremother; he couldn't
help himself. Any number of saints
withdraw from the world. Attila
slaughters three households, Countess Báthory
her own. Mussolini is reelected,
his supporters overjoyed. Grieving, I see
that the self has become unsupportable: lacking
a parent to become, it so to speak
collapses upward. Now I must post this,
I who was Hegel and Freud.

## Effort

How often (it's a real question)
have I sat on a bed or couch,
one arm or awkwardly both
around someone, or in a facing chair
not touching
while incoherent sobs,
terrible inappropriate
wit, or dulled endless
memory poured out –
not directed at me,
me only there
by chance, the chance of relationship
perhaps, but tangential,
just passing through –
thinking that the limits
of language and/or
compassion are nearer,
narrower than people admit;
and that I will hear the same voice
(who else's?) when the time comes,
offering what help
it can.

## Return to Sender

It's the last village before the mountains.
The usual castle, church, and charm.
A war memorial – a grim bronze boy
plus serviceable plaques for later slaughters,
and something abstract in a traffic circle
to commemorate the plagues. I hadn't
been here an hour when I realized:
they're all young, in couples, and in love.
Not egregious about it – except the two
behind the hotel desk, to whom I
apologized for how I looked and smelled
after several weeks' walking. (The room
and shower are adequate.) They hardly noticed;
and those with hands in each other's rear pockets,
holding hands over tables, kissing at random moments,
straight, gay, complex, all vastly tolerant,
are similarly unaware of me,
though I must be the oldest person here
as well as the most solitary. If
I catch someone alone, I'll ask
what happened to the old, but sense
the answer will be sad, not terrifying.

The food is standard. The waitress
seems bright and brave, self-consciously solo.
There may be signs that, if she has time
after serving couples, she'll ask what I'm writing.
A letter, I'll say, which could raise other questions
such as why I'm doing so quaint a thing,

with such an obsolete technology …
but no. The gentle background music
seems to combine in some new way
in every segment all the songs ever written;
it's like a pheromone. You'd like it.
Tomorrow I start into the highlands.
There the bad weather might begin, the cold;
but you mustn't worry. I think they'd like me more
if they knew I was writing you.
I'll be long gone, of course, when the envelope
returns to this hotel (the address I'll give),
somewhat creased perhaps, with stamps saying there's
no longer such a person, or never was.

## February

A bough of some leafy evergreen
a yard from the house, extending
far from the compact mass
of its plant, seems
alone to be affected
by the wind. It nods and nods
and twists and waves
wildly, seeking the window;
like someone talking, complaining
with his hands, head, whole body,
not expecting to be heard.

Maybe an ancestor.

I find myself making the gesture,
easily ignored or, if need be,
denied – hand flat, palm down,
as if patting
air – that I make
when someone's too loud.

## Vigil

When night falls, I chip away
at the stone. Dust fills the air,
but one thing everyone has
is masks. Then I perform
observances I won't describe, then write
in the diary. Longhand.
(Instead of blithering for an hour, take
an hour between each sentence and the next.)
Then neatening, a last candle. Sometimes
the anger comes, but I've noticed how,
if focused on,
the slightest creak suppresses it.
By now it's often dawn ...
I envy the sleepers; you could say
I bless them, if they *are* asleep.
If happiness, as the text says,
exists but not for us,
who is it for? And is it valid?

## The Fighting Starts

A noted playwright from a future era
bases a piece
on ours. The costumes,
initially mud-brown sackcloth
to indicate these people are the dead,
are in later acts the black tunics
of willful or desperate action – both
traditional elements. (This playwright,
though often quirky,
is very much a traditionalist.)
Light is dim and even; dialogue,
apportioned to all forces, fragmentary.
Among the mob – who are not,
though decayed by the end, primarily
the poor – some carry rods
(one knows what these mean), and
perform much comic business as they kill.
(The poor are lightly suggested.)
The scholar's single tear
as they mass, conventionally the highpoint,
is interestingly parodied or echoed
by an elevated stationary figure.

The hanamachi, retained
from an old, contributory form
(a ramp, down which traditionally
the hero, sleeves flying, features
resolved, contorted, stomped), at the end remains empty
though the audience waits and waits. This causes
talk, on which the author
won't waste expensive air.

**Thy Tent**

The figure who, they would tell you, led them here
("they" being their mothers in the dreamtime)
is a vivid myth pileup:
Freud's primal sociopathic patriarch,
but instead of occasioning religion he
invented it. Had a vision
of another place – of course it had to be
across, within, the desert. Took them there.
Their feelings for him are unclear.
Never raped or beaten, they nonetheless dream
of violence, then give thanks
(it's self-congratulation more than prayer)
for being, each morning, where they are.
For hard grain hard to thresh. For streams
and ditches. For lizards
and berries, well-tended
weeds that keep the sand at bay,
backs strong though stooped.

Loves brief and febrile, or constant, sinking
into but sweetening the chronic silence.
Few scheduled, many ad hoc festivals
where jewelry is worn and things
unspoken shouted, danced, or chanted.
Men, who appear in dreams, are measured
against the prophet (Did he, in fact,
exist? his image does) and both
found wanting; if yearning persists,
a well-worn meditation buries it:

*Desire is probably error.*
More pressing through the long hot days
is to keep one's linen not too loosely wound,
neck firm beneath its basket, eyes
shaded. To an impossible stranger
they would seem white shadows walking in white haze.

Yet they endure:
lonely and thirsty
girls come from the desert or are found there.

## Stately Home

A tale of redemption, the "change of heart"
that, once inserted, ruins any plot.
The scandal, trial, and outraged verdict
erased the Bentleys and the household staff;
left him and the third wife (who
had no place left to go)
one floor of the mildewed wing
where the books were. (Domestically
they achieved what could be called
a mutual neutralization
of poisons.) Remaining funds
spiffed up the rest of the House;
when sober, he stood in doorways observing
workmen restoring. Then kids
from the National Trust, well-briefed
and professionally earnest, led
tours; he and his wife appeared
at the end to smile and chat. (Among
the books he read in desperation
was an old novel by some Indian
about a thief who hides in a disused temple,
pretending to be, eventually becoming
holy.) Behind the smile he looked
at the tourists – proles, chancers, tired
faces seeking something
probably specious – and thought that
behind a life lies what's behind
a stage: other people working.

## Session

When Talleyrand died, Metternich
said, "Why did he do that?"
But the cunning of this aged writer
housed all day in a doubtful armchair
is greater still – he projects
posthumous triumph
on the basis of a work
like the one Benjamin wanted, entirely composed
of quotations. Will start
with Nietzsche: "Fifty years after my death,
when I have become a myth ... "
(how does the rest go?). Cleverly segue
to brilliant lost acquaintances
from the old days: Greg R.: "Some go to school,
some think they're smart 'cause they don't go to school,
and some say 'Jesus Jesus Jesus.'" Samantha
W.: "Show me the road
to freedom and I'll show you a maze." (Or was it
"maturity"?) But a memory
hobbles him: he and Sam
agreeing, not even stoned, one afternoon
that the last line of that Kosinski novel
("One orgasm more or less – what's the difference?")
was the most depressing in all fiction.

## Request

I want to see the sky in four billion years.
The Andromeda Galaxy angled across
the night, its disc beginning
to fray, to admit
ours. I know this couch,
etc., will be unavailable;
maybe someplace nearby ... I also
know, quite well, that
a wish may be impossible though moderate.

## Late Period

History per se
didn't interest him. History is a bull
who imagines himself a matador.
Art is the matador, whose job is
to serve up horned skulls.
Towards the end he walked Kabul,
his Afghan (whose features
he assimilated to Jacqueline's) on
the beach. There he met hippies.
The girls and sometimes the boys adored
the dog. They were often madly
dressed and accoutered; generally
Americans, who are anyway big and absurd.
Some knew who he was and struggled
to find something to say, but said it
in English. Others seemed too
proud in the face of status
to do more than laze. All vividly
doomed. In his studio,
he assimilated them to
hidalgos of the Siglo de Oro –
stoned if only on tobacco;
pleased for the moment
with their flaring collars, plumes, lace, swords, and pipes.

## The Liberator

The features reveal nothing: young, polite
white guy. What he *does* is unclear;
what it means is we won't have to fight.
At first he talked to people, one on one,
in the Midwest somewhere.
Then came the new, then older media,
and they fell asleep. Those who would block
abortion clinic entrances
or rally, march, shoot, bomb, harass,
just snore, laptops and rifles within reach,
their televisions off, kids unabused.
Some can be roused, eat rather vacantly
then doze again; but major
backers, donors, spiritual leaders,
owners can't. And everywhere, on cots,
in hammocks, watched by bemused
child soldiers or on billion-dollar yachts,
that sort of person sleeps. Unmenaced, teachers
teach. New housing rises, old
is repaired. (Some mansions, once
the limp are warehoused, get repurposed.)
Unions expand and take initiatives;
doctors – well, we have to keep those people
alive, don't we? – take to the skies
internationally, with glucose ...
Whoever you are, you can walk at night,
anywhere.

He agrees to a meeting
in the auditorium of a former
corporate tower. One representative
asks how he can understand Black anguish
(which is quantified at length). "I probably can't,
emotionally, but I sympathize."
But can you *understand* it? Someone else
demands if he knows how, e.g., the child bride
in an arranged marriage feels when the man is ...
absent. "Better?" he suggests,
which causes turmoil. A comparable
contretemps when he admits
in passing to being straight. Voices accuse him
of authoritarian leanings.
"Do you want me to reawaken them?"
he asks with his usual lack
of stress. They turn on each other.
I hang around; when they're mostly gone,
I invite him for a drink.
The affect doesn't change, though he seems tired.
"In my experience, I've noticed that,
whatever love or tolerance you have,
to talk to fools is to talk down to them."

## The New Cool

Bed, outlets, desk, john, shower, microwave,
small fridge. Some protest:
a chair? Sit on bed, desk your lap.
Issue of roommates, privacy as privilege.
For items six and seven: dumpsters.
Prepare for a bucket to replace item four.
All you need is air, light, water, heat,
laptop, burner phones, and gun.
During the last storm (short for megastorm)
cracks appeared in the Wall and all remaining
able-bodied were called in to help ...
but since there is no Wall as yet
I've done more work on the apartment.
Finished soundproofing. Materials hard
to come by; don't fully
drown the music and hysterias
of all the ethnicities and genders
(each still superior to the rest) who have
been siphoned to this part of town.
By day I organize, get beaten up,
though progressively less.
By night C., not her real initial,
drops by; we're militant together.
Dawn light, my only artwork, curled
for a moment across the ceiling, I remake
the bed (with military corners),
make coded calls re coming actions,
and plan the postwar world.

# Selected Poetry Titles Published by SurVision Books

**Contemporary Tangential Surrealist Poetry: An Anthology**
Edited by Tony Kitt
ISBN 978-1-912963-44-7

**Invasion: An Anthology of Ukrainian Poetry about the War**
Edited by Tony Kitt
ISBN 978-1-912963-32-4

**Noelle Kocot.** *Humanity*
(New Poetics: USA)
ISBN 978-1-9995903-0-7

**Marc Vincenz.** *Einstein Fledermaus*
(New Poetics: USA)
ISBN 978-1-912963-20-1

**Helen Ivory.** *Maps of the Abandoned City*
(New Poetics: England)
ISBN 978-1-912963-04-1

**Tony Kitt.** *The Magic Phlute*
(New Poetics: Ireland)
ISBN 978-1-912963-08-9

**Clayre Benzadón.** *Liminal Zenith*
(New Poetics: USA)
ISBN 978-1-912963-11-9

**Thomas Townsley.** *Tangent of Ardency*
(New Poetics: USA)
ISBN 978-1-912963-15-7

**Mikko Harvey & Jake Bauer.** *Idaho Falls*
(Winner of James Tate Poetry Prize 2018)
ISBN 978-1-912963-02-7

**John Bradley.** *Spontaneous Mummification*
(Winner of James Tate Poetry Prize 2019)
ISBN 978-1-912963-13-3

**Charles Kell.** *Pierre Mask*
(Winner of James Tate Poetry Prize 2019)
ISBN 978-1-912963-19-5

**Charles Borkhuis.** *Spontaneous Combustion*
(Winner of James Tate Poetry Prize 2021)
ISBN 978-1-912963-30-0

**Noah Falck and Matt McBride.** *Prerecorded Weather*
(Winner of James Tate Poetry Prize 2022)
ISBN 978-1-912963-39-3

**Jeffrey Cyphers Wright.** *Fuel for Love*
(Winner of James Tate Poetry Prize 2023)
ISBN 978-1-912963-45-4

**George Kalamaras.** *That Moment of Wept*
ISBN 978-1-9995903-7-6

**George Kalamaras.** *Through the Silk-Heavy Rains*
ISBN 978-1-912963-28-7

**Guillaume Apollinaire.** *Ocean of Earth: Selected Poems*
Translated from French by Matthew Geden
ISBN 978-1-912963-40-9

Order our books from survisionmagazine.com

www.ingramcontent.com/pod-product-compliance
Lightning Source LLC
Chambersburg PA
CBHW071947100426
42736CB00042B/2313